THE DECK BOOK

We hope this book inspires you to build your little piece of heaven.....outdoors !

Introduction

Welcome to our new Hickory Dickory Decks ideas and inspirations book. This year we are celebrating our 25th anniversary of custom deck building in Canada and the United States. When I first started the business in 1987, I had no idea that it would become my lifelong career. Along the way, I have met thousands of great customers and would like to think that, in a small way, I have helped enrich each of their lives by providing them with an outdoor living space where they can unwind with family and friends and enjoy a cool beverage after a long day's work.

The deck industry has changed tremendously over the past 25 years . Gone are the days of the rectangular pressure treated platforms, void of any attributes other than a few steps and a couple of lawn chairs for seating. Today, we at Hickory Dickory Decks like to think of our customers' projects as nothing less than an architectural extension of their home's interior living space transplanted outdoors.

When planning an attractive, functional deck design for your property, we need to take into consideration a number of factors. We ask you how you envision using the area. What activities will be done on the deck? What furniture and accessories will be on the deck? If it is a custom deck that will be used for many years, these activities will evolve and change over time as well. You will also want to know how much sun or shade will reach the desired location of the deck. Is privacy or wind an issue ? We help design your deck according to local building code requirements. In Ontario for example, a deck over 24 inches above grade requires a 36" handrail . Again this handrail will have its own set of specifications which will have to be met. Another factor you must consider is property grade. Once the height above grade is over 6 feet, the rail must be raised to 42". These questions and answers are necessary in order to protect yourself from a lawsuit but more importantly to ensure your own safety as well as your guests' safety. As you can see, deciding on using a reputable contractor like Hickory Dickory Decks will take all the worry out of the entire equation.

If you decide to fore-go a contractor and build the project yourself, our sister company H.D.D. Wholesale would be happy to quote on supplying all your decking materials. In over 50 cities in Ontario, we have one of our trucks delivering decking materials weekly. We also ship deck products across Canada and into the United States. H.D.D. Wholesale can be reached at 1-800-263-4774.

Opposite :
A unique deck for a unique property.

Right :
By incorporating a simple curve you make the ordinary extraordinary.

Opposite :
Never underestimate the allure of well maintained plant life in and around your deck.

This new book is full of hundreds of photos which cover a wide spectrum of styles, materials and design needs. We at Hickory Dickory Decks have long realized the power of photography. As the old adage says, "a picture is worth a thousand words". Taking images of our projects has not only been a labor of love for myself but also my good friend Drew Cunningham. Prior to starting with Hickory Dickory Decks eight years ago, Drew worked as a professional photographer with Getty Images News Bureau, New York. During this time he also ran his own small photography studio in downtown Toronto. In addition to his photographic contributions, Drew has helped Hickory Dickory Decks with the development of our global web presence while also providing innovative copy and marketing solutions. To see thousands of additional deck pictures from Drew, our Hickory Dickory Decks team members and franchises, please visit www.decks.ca, www.hickorydickorydecks.com and www.hickorydickorydecks.ca.

Hickory Dickory Decks has over 20 years of experience working with specialized non wood low maintenance decking. We have been there since the beginning, thus our knowledge in this area is unsurpassed. If you don't want slivers, cracked or splitting railings, the occasional warped deck board plus the time and expense of staining your deck each spring then you should be giving us a call. We at Hickory Dickory Decks stock over twenty great products. For 2013, we have teamed up with Clubhouse Decking. They also partnered with us in the production of this book. Visit their website www.deceuninck-americas.com/clubhouse-decking/ and find out why we at Hickory Dickory Decks love showing this product to our clients.

Drew and I have decided to not comment on every picture shown in our new book I hope you enjoy your time looking at our decks and I hope it leads to a new fantastic outdoor living environment at your home for you and your family to enjoy long into the future !

I would like to close by thanking all our fantastic customers for their business, and especially those homeowners who allowed us to use their deck photos as part of this project. Thanks again for your time and if I can help in anyway, please write or call.

Yours truly,

Tom Jacques

President & C.E.O.
Hickory Dickory Decks

Spread :
A lovely integration of both stone and decking creates a unique outdoor living space.

Right :
Great place to read a book and catch a few rays.

Opposite :
The gentle incline of these stairs invite you to the backyard.

Opposite :
This multi - tiered deck is just perfect for a gathering with all your friends.

Below :
Tempered glass, in place of traditional spindles, offers optimal views.

Opposite :
The curved stairs help to accentuate the curve of the pool.

Opposite :
A one of a kind design! Notice the poured concrete base supporting the gazebo.

Opposite :
Waterfront living located in Maine, USA.

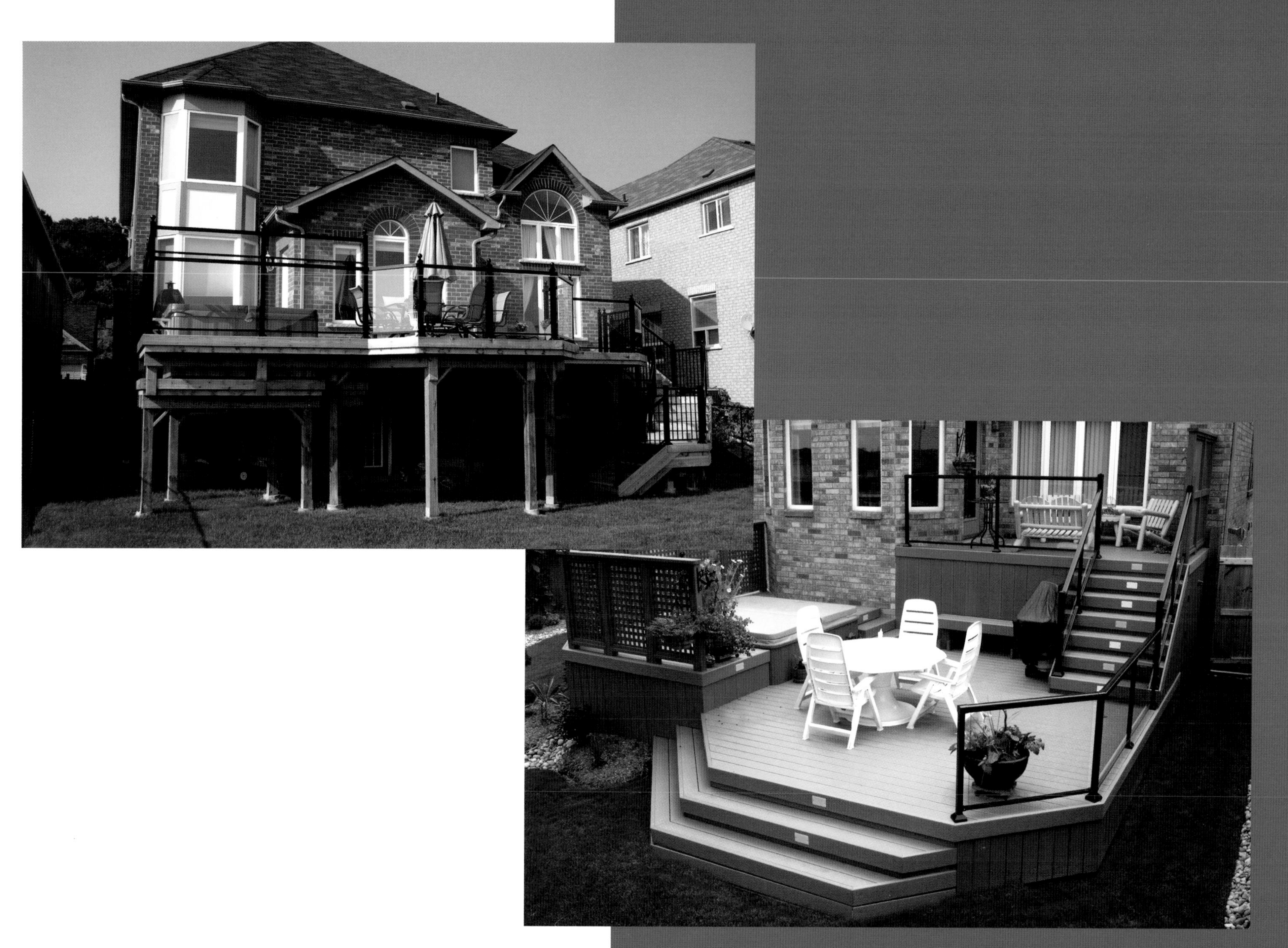

Opposite :
The stone skirting of the deck is a perfect match with the stonework of the home.

Opposite :
A great place to make new friends !

Right:
A cozy retreat to catch up at the end of a busy day.

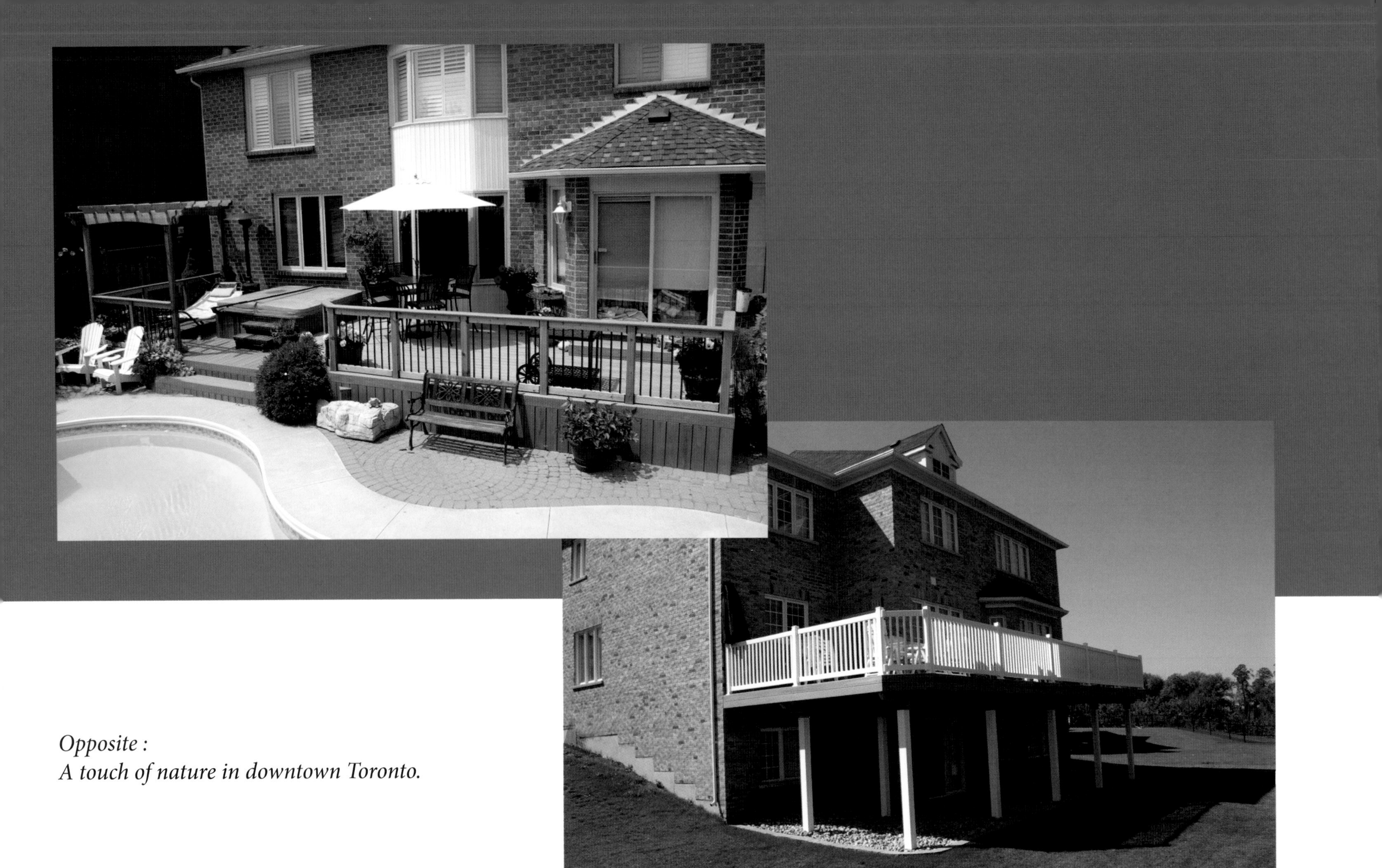

Opposite :
A touch of nature in downtown Toronto.

Top :
A little light provides a relaxing ambiance at dusk.

Opposite :
A great build in London, Ontario.

Spread:
This grand deck measures over 1400 square ft in size

Top:
Utilizing another colour helps accentuate the geometric shape of this unique deck.

Opposite :
A hardwood deck complemented by a built in stone fire pit.

Opposite :
A grand elevated deck offers spectacular views of the surrounding area.

Right :
Built in Toronto in 1988.

Opposite :
A screened in area offers refuge from springtime bugs.

Right :
The beauty of lake country, Maine USA.

Right :
The stone columns match perfectly with the home's facade.

Opposite :
Two mediums, rock and decking, joined together to make one handsome outdoor living area.

Opposite :
A great example of the use of two distinct mediums.

Top :
Winter in Maine, USA.

Opposite :
Another great example of a semi circle making the average deck all the more special!

Top :
This gazebo was made with Brazilian hardwood. This wood will last for years.

Opposite :
A well designed deck addition can look as if it is part of the original home.

Right :
Night lights on the steps make for a safer environment.

Opposite :
Creative lighting concepts only accentuate a deck's appeal.

Top :
A steel substructure will last a lifetime.

Spread :
This is truly a grand property. The all stone home is accented by the matching stone deck and solid stone bar. This home would make even the most discriminating owner proud !

Right :
A large Clubhouse party deck with wonderful views of the surrounding area.

Opposite :
This cedar deck is perfect for small to large gatherings.

Right:
A very creative use of curves accentuates this deck's design.

Spread :
A granite laicea deck enclosed by an intricate aluminum privacy screen.

Below :
Tempered glass, instead of spindles, allows unobstructed views.

Opposite :
A wonderful screened in gazebo and large deck offers grand views!

Right :
A portable shelter helps keep the bugs away on those spring days.

Opposite :
Anyone for a cool dip ?

This page :
Great views and room to relax on this Clubhouse party deck.

Opposite:
A nice curved bench follows the curve of the deck.

ROOTS
ROOTS

Right :
Hickory Dickory Decks' first deck built at our head office in Flamborough, Ont.

This page :
Lounge chairs truly turns this outdoor deck into an extension of interior living!

Left :
Relaxing under a rainbow, what more could you want?

Opposite :
A traditional raised deck in Kitchener, Ontario.

Right :
A stunning balcony offering fantastic views of the surrounding countryside.

Left :
A cozy deck in Sudbury, Ontario.

Below :
A set of stairs with a gentle incline.

Right :
Take a moment and relax!

Opposite :
A grand elevated deck with a nice spindle railing system.

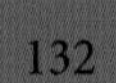

Opposite :
A grand multi level deck with built in hot tub is the ultimate in luxury living.

Left :
A well built bench for three.

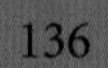

Left :
A stone fireplace and the creative use of lighting, creates an inviting area to relax.

Left :
A beautiful curved iron rod railing resting atop 8 x 8 pillars.

Below :
Sometimes bigger is better!

Top :
Anyone for a cool drink?

Opposite :
In order to keep the large tree, the decking was cut to fit around the tree's trunk.

Left :
A nice combination of decking and various stone work make this little deck a real beauty.

Opposite :
The whole gang gather to say "cheez" for the camera on the steps of this spacious Clubhouse party deck.

Opposite :
Ample lighting makes for a great place for after hours socializing.

Left :
A diamond shaped accent was made in this deck by the careful placement of complimentary colour decking.

Opposite :
A great customer and friend takes a break next to his new outdoor living space.

Opposite :
The curve of the deck follows the outline of the pool nicely.

Spread :
Truly a grand deck to behold!

Opposite :
Cedar and low maintenance decking were used on this project.

20 61

Left :
This little gem was built in Petrolia, Ontario.

Top :
A screened in cabana extends your spring days into comfortable evenings.

Top :
Though hard to construct, this circular designed deck turned out nicely.

Opposite :
This deck makes good use of an alternate colour to act as trim.

Below :
Hot dog anyone ?

Opposite :
This grand deck is located on the shores of Lake Huron, Ontario.

Spread :
The river rock bordering this deck is a nice touch.

Spread :
This deck was constructed with beautiful Clubhouse decking.

Opposite :
The curved balcony sits elegantly over the lush landscape below.

Below :
This elevated deck offers beautiful fall views.

Spread :
This deck with its use of numerous materials is truly an architectural dream !